Pam

By Bernie Feldstein

Illustrated by Sheila Bailey

Target Skill Setting

PEARSON

Scott
Foresman

I am Pam.

Here is my dog, Rex.

I will fix my black truck.

Rex and I will ride in my black truck.

Here is my hen, Trix.

Trix will go for a ride too.

Here is my big ox, Max.